QUILT AS YOU GO MADE EASY

Complete step by step instructions with pictures on how to quilt as you go

Lucy Gabriel

Table of content

Chapter One

Introduction to Quilt As You Go

Sewing is something that I
totally enjoy.I'm an amateur
yet, so it's continually testing

and fun and imaginative at the same time. The one issue I have, notwithstanding, with each blanket I make, is the way that it is terrible difficult to machine quilt on your standard, average sewing machine. It's a goliath exercise, continually pushing, pulling, and attempting to monitor a major folded up hunk of blanket pushed into a customary estimated sewing machine. As much as I would do pretty much anything for one of those goliath, insane marvelous since quite a while ago outfitted sewing machines explicitly implied for stitching, I'm not actually feeling that will happen any time soon. (That is to say, truly, what's with these children expecting to eat constantly? They are absolutely slaughtering my sewing machine dreams!)

So as I was looking for a superior answer for my stitching issue, I ran over knitting as you go. The fundamental thought is to stitch the entirety of your layers together, as you are piecing your blanket, so you are working with more modest, more sensible pieces. There are a wide range of ways you can do this, yet the fundamental thought is all basically the equivalent: you stack your pieced block, with batting and sponsorship slice to a similar size, sandwich them together and quilt them first, and afterward really consolidate blocks.

Chapter Two

Instructions to follow

Stage 1: Make a Plan

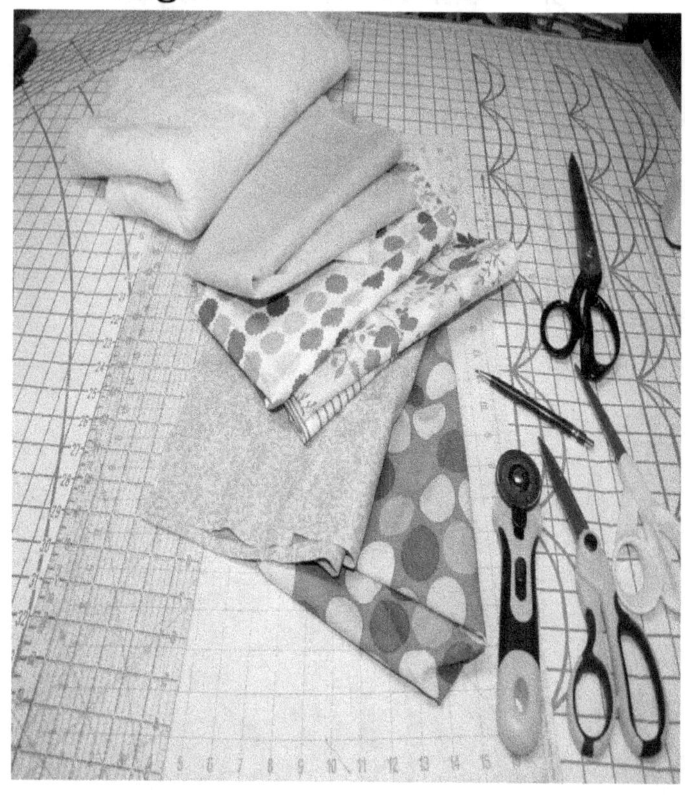

The initial step is to make an arrangement. Choose the size and plan the design that you might want your completed work to be, and sort out the yardage you would require for that size. This would go pretty also to your standard blanket undertaking, the solitary contrast would be is that your support will

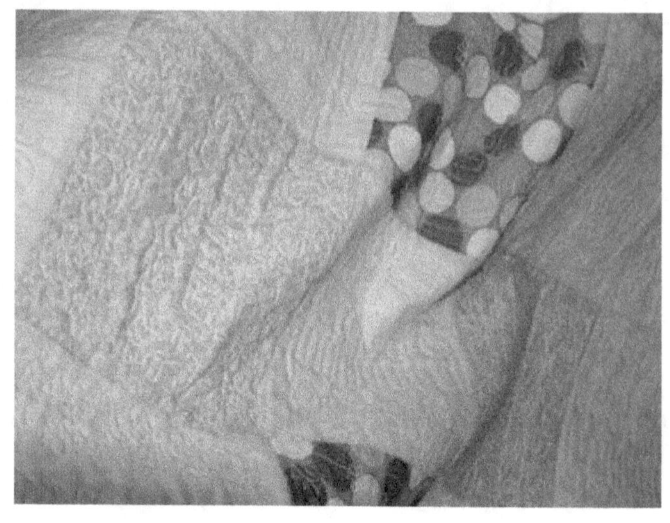

all be pieced, so it won't be

important to have straig

yardage for your project.

Chapter Three

Stage 2: Sizing Your Blocks, Batting and Back

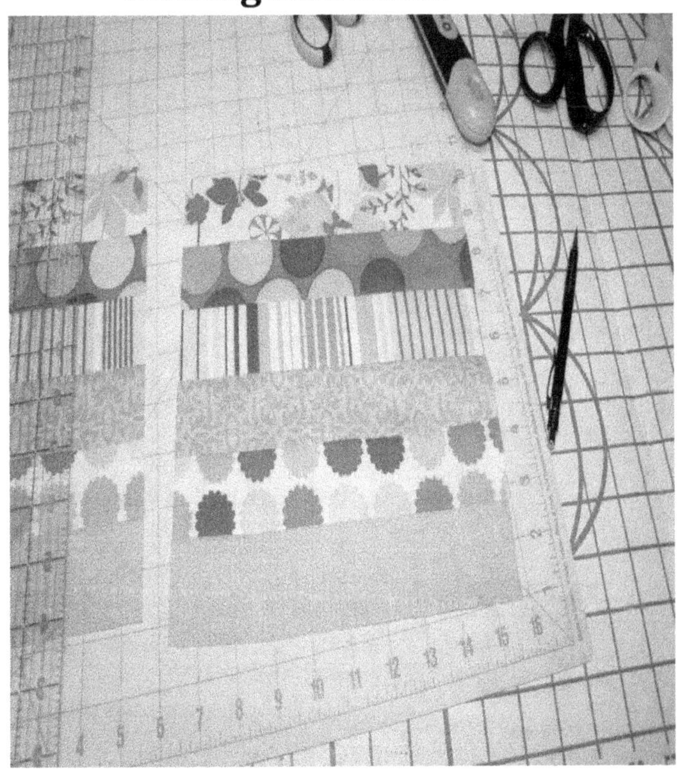

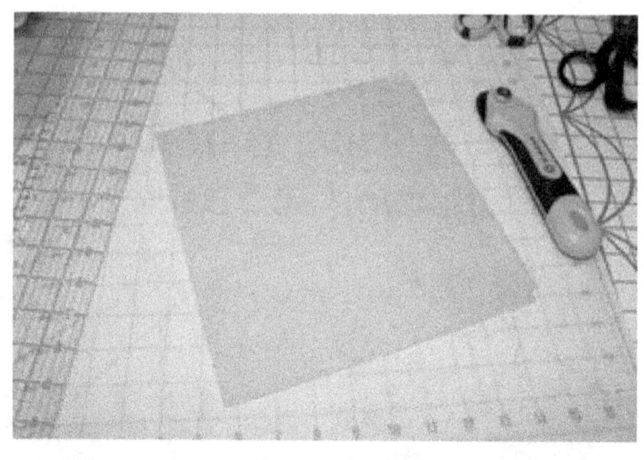

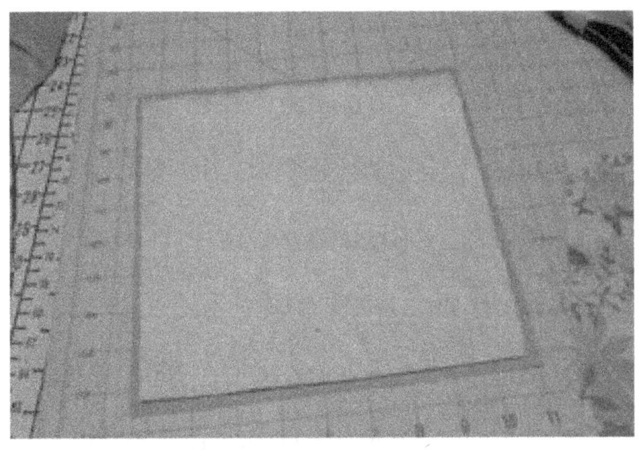

For this task, I chose to make
an infant measured quilt, around
36" x 45". My plan utilized 4
squares across, and 5 lines,
which were all 9" completed
size. I will utilize this for
instance, however you can
actually use various
sizes/examples to work inside
your task.

When I pieced my top squares, I trimmed them to be 9" PLUS crease stipend. I would truly suggest utilizing at least half of an inch around each side of each square. (I just utilized ¼", and made me absolutely bonkers and didn't work out just as I would have enjoyed.)

At the point when you have your top squares trimmed, you should manage backing squares to be precisely the same size as the top.

When you have your top and support cut, slice your batting to estimate. This part is somewhat unique... you need your batting to not have any crease stipend whatsoever. In the event that batting is running into your crease, you'll have considerably an excess of mass in your creases. For instance, in my blanket, my batting squares were every 9" even.

Chapter Four

Stage 3: Make a Sammich.

When you have all of your squares pieced and trimmed to measure, you need to stack your sandwiches.

To stack them, you should begin by laying your supporting fabric, wrong side up, on your work surface.

On top of this, place your batting square. Try to put it in the middle, with allowance on the line of stitching around each side.

When you have your batting put, place your top square over it, straight up. Make certain to fix it up cautiously with your support square underneath.

At the point when you have the entire layers position, you need to stitch them. You can simply pin them, as I have done, or spray stitch... whatever takes care of the work. Typically I do not like using straight pins to stitch a quilt, yet these little squares require so minimal that it is anything but a serious deal to me.

Stage 4: Quilt!

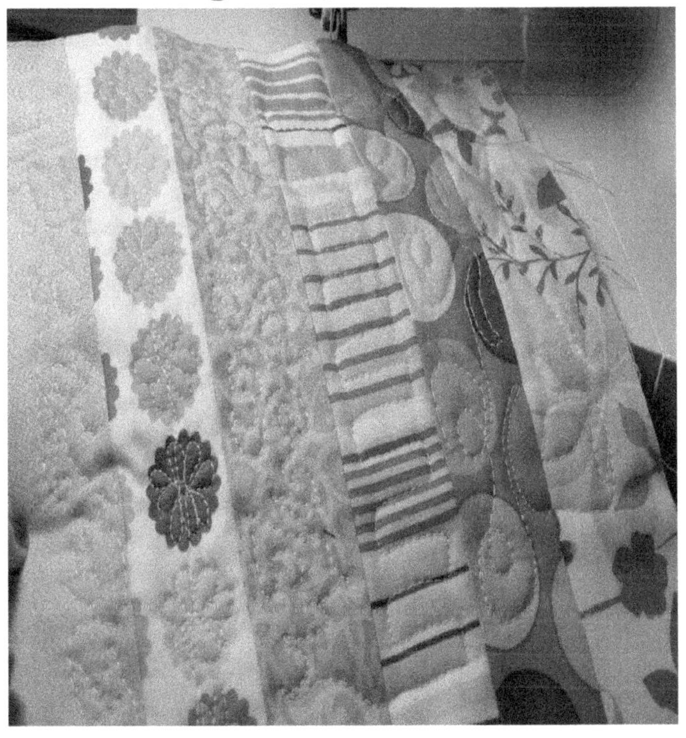

once you have your layers
stitched, you should knit your
squares.

How you quilt your squares is totally up to you. You can utilize straight lines or freestyle quilt it... essentially do whatever you are generally OK with. The main thing to recall is to not sew into your line of stitching allowance. I did this in a couple of spots, and it was a major torment in the backside in later advances. You can also use a marking pencil that is easily erase and

mark around the edges so you realize where to stop.

Chapter Five

Stage 5: Joining Your Blocks

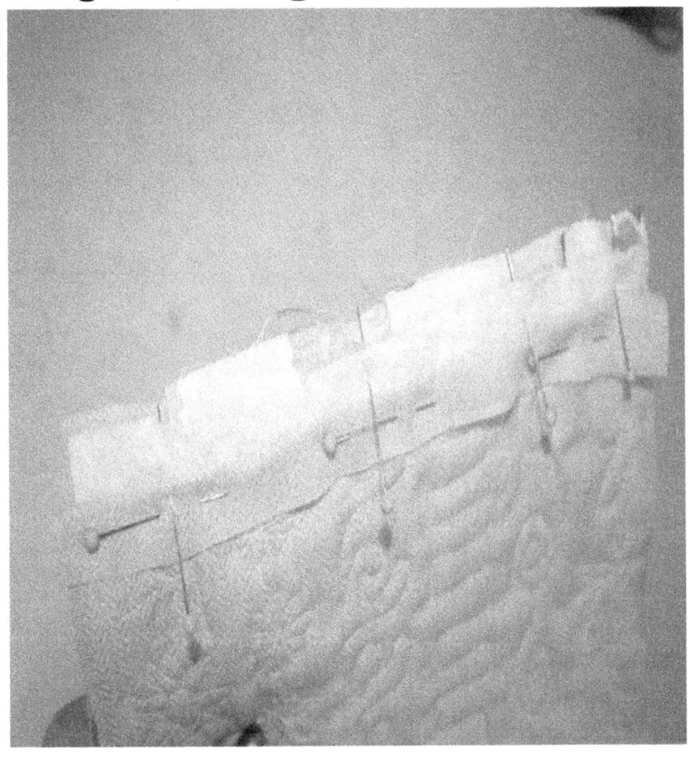

When you have a large stack of stitched squares, you really will start combining them together.

To join squares, place two squares, right sides together. Carefully pin JUST the top layers together. You would prefer not to sew through your supporting fabric . I thought that it was most straightforward to one or the other pin or press the pulling out of the way while I sewed the tops together.

Stage 6: Press Your Seam

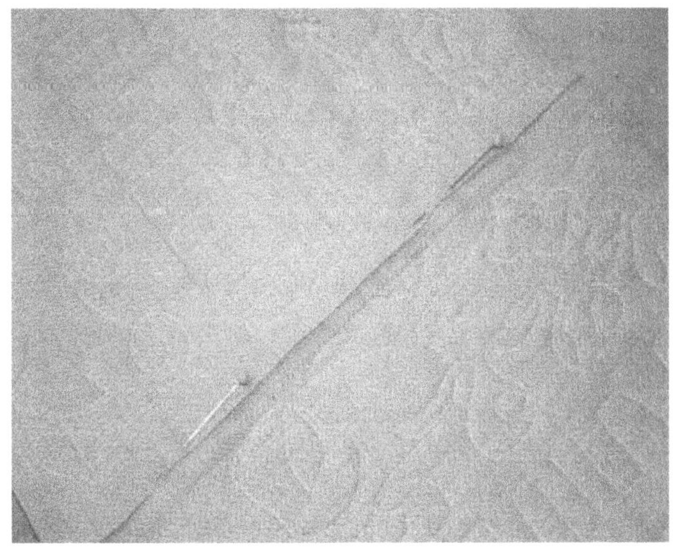

When you get the two squares joined exactly at the top layer, press your stitch. At that point smooth the supporting fabric back over the back of the stitch, folding more than one edge and sticking.

Stage 7: Finishing Your Back seam

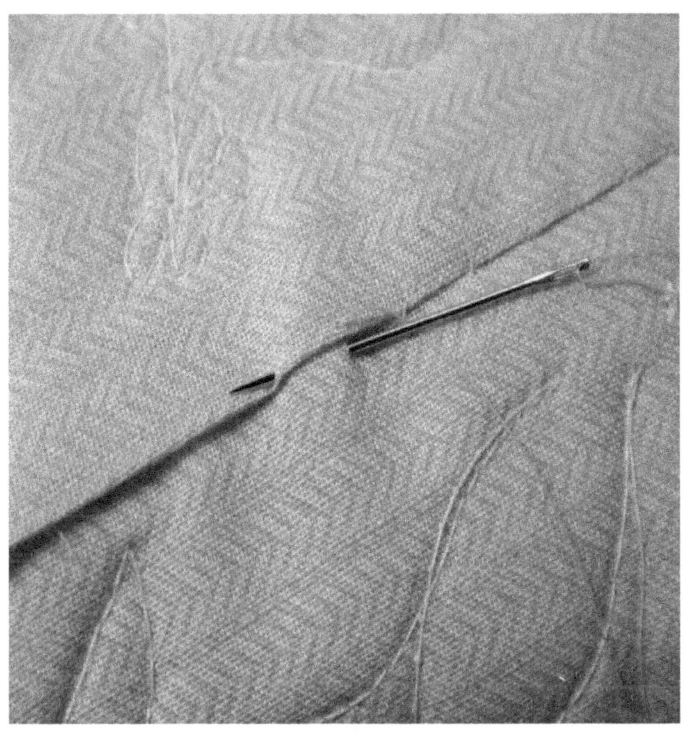

At the point when you have your column[rolls] all joined, you need to return and complete your back stitch. You could, carefully, line up and pin your supporting fabric a machine join everything down. I decided to line this by hand, since I didn't need the whine of concealing seams and arranging things perfectly. I stitched as perfectly and as undetectably as could reasonably be expected, and for me, it was simpler.

I would suggest that as you stitch your back, try not to leave your seams open on the top and base, so when you combine your lines, you will have the option to open your layers straight across.

Chapter Six

Stage 8: Join Your Rows!

At the point when you have the entire of your lines stitch, you can sew them together utilizing the very procedures that you used to join your squares into columns[rows]. What's more, similarly as you completed the back of each row, finish the seams that you use to combine the columns together.

Chapter Seven

Stage 9: Finish It!

that is the fundamental idea!

When you have your quilt

assembled, you tie it similarly as you would a regular quilt.

Stage 10:

This method is so easy, and it truly opens up alot of opportunities for more complex quilting design plans on an essential model sewing machine. I could even see doing a lot bigger undertakings than what I am utilized to, since I won't need to stress over compelling a full measured blanket through my machine. It is additionally loans to scrap quilts, which are consistently fun and an extraordinary method to go through fabric that you've had

laying around for some time.